HOW DO I BECOME A . . . ?

TV Reporter

Mindi Rose Englart

Photographs by Peter Casolino & Melanie Stengel

BLACKBIRCH®
PRESS

THOMSON
★
GALE

San Diego • Detroit • New York • San Francisco • Cleveland • New Haven, Conn. • Waterville, Maine • London • Munich

THOMSON

GALE

© 2003 by Blackbirch Press™. Blackbirch Press™ is an imprint of The Gale Group, Inc., a division of Thomson Learning, Inc.

Blackbirch Press™ and Thomson Learning™ are trademarks used herein under license.

For more information, contact
The Gale Group, Inc.
27500 Drake Rd.
Farmington Hills, MI 48331-3535
Or you can visit our Internet site at http://www.gale.com

Photo Credits: All photos © Peter Casolino and Melanie Stengel

LIBRARY OF CONGRESS CATALOGING-IN-PUBLICATION DATA

Englart, Mindi Rose.
  TV reporter / by Mindi Rose Englart.
    v. cm. — (How do I become a: series)
  Includes index.
  Contents: Becoming a TV reporter — A college education — Using the camera — On the air — On the job.
    ISBN 1-56711-419-9 (hardback : alk. paper)
  1. Television broadcasting of news—Vocational guidance—Juvenile literature. 2. Reporters and reporting—Vocational guidance—Juvenile literature.
  [1. Television broadcasting of news—Vocational guidance. 2. Reporters and reporting—Vocational guidance. 3. Vocational guidance.] I. Title. II. Series.

PN4784.T4 E54 2003
070.4′3′023—dc21   2002013545

Printed in China
10 9 8 7 6 5 4 3 2 1

CONTENTS

Dedication
To my Aunt Toby

Special Thanks
The publisher and the author would like to thank the following people for their participation in this project: Sue Bradley, Joanie Lincoln, Ron Zorn, Jim Robinson, Connecticut School of Broadcasting and Robinson Media; Jon Hitchcock, Virginia Fisher, Veronica Douglas, and the staff at News Channel 8 in New Haven, Connecticut; and Jerry Dunklee at Southern Connecticut State University. The author would also like to thank editors Claire Kreger and Janet Reed Blake.

If you would like more information about the organizations featured in this book, visit www.800tvradio.com, www.wtnh.com, or www.southernct.edu

▲ **TV reporters tell people about important events and information**

Television reporters sit at a desk and tell their viewers about the day's events. They want to make a difference in the world by giving people information. They report important news and also provide information on the weather and sports. They may also present stories about interesting people or go to the scene of a crime or a fire. A lot goes into each broadcast. Presenting the news on TV is only one step in a TV reporter's job.

How does a person become a TV reporter?

Good TV reporters learn how to ▲
think quickly under pressure and
perform well in front of a camera.

Qualities of a TV Reporter

Reporters are naturally curious people. They are interested in the world around them. They must be able to talk to all kinds of people. They must be able to put together a news story that is clear and accurate. Lots of people want to work in this exciting field. The competition makes it hard to become a TV reporter. Those who make it on TV must have a lot of skills, personality, and a little luck. Most importantly, people need to be good writers and storytellers.

Sometimes viewers do not give their full attention to the television. A TV reporter must tell an interesting story so people watch them. TV reporters always start and end a broadcast by saying their name and the news organization they work for.

TV reporters must be able to think quickly and perform in front of a camera. They do research for their stories and read a lot to learn about current events. News changes throughout the day. Sometimes a story gets canceled because another news story may seem more important. A good reporter must be able to quickly prepare a news story.

▲ **On camera, a reporter must not let feelings get in the way of reporting a story.**

TV reporters work long hours. They often work nights, weekends, and holidays—when people in most other jobs are off. Reporters must always be ready to get to work on a story. Sometimes TV reporters cover events that make them sad or angry. They must be able to do their job and not let their feelings get in the way of reporting the news clearly.

News anchors host daily ▲
news shows from a studio.

Types of TV Reporters

There are many types of TV reporters. One type of reporter is a news anchor. News anchors host daily news shows from a studio. Anchors report news and also introduce other TV reporters throughout the broadcast. Many TV reporters work to become anchors.

Another type of TV reporter is a field reporter. This kind of reporter covers stories at the location where they happen. There are also sports, education, and health reporters. Investigative reporters do research on important issues and present their findings to viewers. They often have more time to put their stories together than other reporters. Feature reporters work on stories about interesting people.

Trade School

Some students may go to special trade schools, such as the Connecticut School of Broadcasting (CSB) in Farmington, Connecticut. At CSB, students take 112 hours of classes. They learn all the steps involved in television reporting.

**Students can learn aspects of broadcasting
▼ at trade schools, such as CSB.**

FACT: LARGE TELEVISION STATIONS USUALLY USE THREE STUDIO CAMERAS FOR A NEWS BROADCAST. A BIG EVENT, SUCH AS THE SUPERBOWL, MAY USE TWENTY-FIVE CAMERAS!

A College Education

These days, it's very important to have a college education to get hired as a TV reporter. Some people choose to get a four-year degree in communications or journalism. These programs teach students all forms of journalism (gathering, writing, and reporting news). Students who major in broadcast journalism get technical training on the equipment used to make a TV news show. They may even have access to a college TV station. This gives students the chance to practice their skills at school.

In college, students learn to do research and to write well. Some students choose to learn about a variety of subjects—from history to political science and the arts. Students also take classes in math, science, and English.

Journalism students take field trips to radio and TV stations. At these stations, they talk to experienced reporters and ask questions about the job. Students also watch TV news shows. Teachers talk about what the news shows do well and what they could do differently. Students learn the history of broadcasting. They learn how people have passed on information throughout history and how this led to reporting on television.

Many students choose to get a ▶ college degree in journalism before starting their career.

Students study how the law impacts TV reporting. They learn that they must report news in an accurate and fair way. They also learn about the First Amendment to the Constitution, which says that all Americans have the right to free speech. This gives journalists the right to report on any subject they feel is important. Not all countries give journalists this freedom.

In school, students learn all aspects ▲
of running a TV show, including the
machines in the control room.

Learning to Write for TV

In some ways, writing a TV news report is the same as writing any story. Each report needs a beginning, a middle, and an end. But there are a number of things that make writing for TV news special. For example, a TV story may need to be told in only one and a half minutes. Also, TV news stories must be finished within strict deadlines.

TV reporters learn to write news stories that go with the video the cameraperson has shot. A TV reporter also needs to get good "sound bites." These are short bits of interviews that give a lot of information in a little time.

Who, What, Where, When, Why—and How

TV reporters interview people, called subjects, to get information for their stories. Therefore, students must learn to interview people well. They learn how to ask the right questions and how to be good listeners.

Students try to answer the six key questions for each story: First, they must decide **who** the story is about. Next, they must tell **what** happened that makes the story important. Then, they must tell **where** and **when** the important event happened and **why** it is important. Finally, students give details about **how** the important event took place. Once student reporters can answer these questions, they can write an interesting story.

Student reporters practice delivering their stories on camera. ▶

Equipment

Students must study the technical parts of TV reporting. For example, students learn how to use a camera. Students learn to focus, tilt, and zoom in on a subject to get a clear shot.

TV crews have special names for how they move a camera. The space between a person's head and the frame of the camera shot is called headroom. It is important to leave at least an inch of headroom above a subject so the head does not look cut off on TV.

Adjusting the microphone ▶

Adjusting the lights ▶

It is important to get the lighting just right. Students learn to control how much light gets into the camera's lens. This lets viewers see details of the scene. Sometimes a cameraperson will need to shine more lights on a subject. Students also learn to adjust microphones so reporters and their subjects will sound their best.

13

An instructor helps a ▲
student learn the proper
way to sit at a news desk.

Looking Good

In order to appeal to their audience, TV reporters must look good on television. Students learn to dress professionally. They must speak clearly and be likeable. They should also have good posture. On camera, people sit close to each other. They must remember to always keep their hands above the desk. Teachers remind students not to tap their feet as they report stories.

Reporters should be relaxed. They must look into the camera and smile. Students learn to breathe deeply using their belly muscles. This can help them feel less nervous. Students also learn other exercises to help them relax. For example, they may pretend they are talking to a good friend instead of hundreds of thousands of viewers.

Students learn to speak at the right volume. Students practice vocal warm-ups. These exercises are words and sentences that help them relax their mouths and speak clearly.

TRY THIS: Try a vocal warm-up. Say the italicized sentence ten times in a row. Focus on saying each word clearly. *Rubber baby buggy bumpers.*

On the Air

Students get to practice being "on the air," which means being on TV. First, they learn to use a very important machine called a teleprompter. A teleprompter is attached to the camera. The words of each story appear on its screen. Reporters read their stories from it. This way, reporters can look into the camera and not forget to say anything important. Reporters also have paper versions of their stories in front of them.

Students learn to focus on the lens of the camera. They practice telling the news at an even pace.

Students learn that before going on the air, everyone in the studio goes through a final check. Reporters check their notes. Camerapeople check the amount of light on the subject. Sound engineers check the volume levels. When it is time to start the broadcast, the floor director says, "Stand by. Quiet on the set." Then the floor director counts down: "Live in five, four, three, two, one."

The floor director speaks to ▶
the director using a headset.

15

Interns get ► on-the-job training before they apply for full-time jobs.

Internship

An internship is on-the-job training. Internships are an important part of training to become a TV reporter. A student can have an internship while in school, or after graduation. Sometimes interns get college credit for working at a station. Internships give students the experience they need to get hired at a TV station. Some people have many internships before they get a job.

Interns at a TV station are supervised by experienced reporters. Interns are not usually paid. They do a little bit of everything—answer phones, file papers, and line up interviews. This helps the station get things done. It also helps interns gain experience. Interns eventually get to research story ideas. They call police departments to see what is happening locally. They also find story ideas on the Internet. If they are lucky, they get to go out in the field with an experienced reporter.

Live Reporting

Reporters go to an event with a cameraperson. For example, they may cover a circus opening or a traffic accident. During sudden news events, TV reporters may not have time to come back to the station to write a story. The reporter may have to quickly jot down some notes and start reporting right away.

A TV reporter will usually ask the cameraperson to start with a wide shot of the location. This is known as the establishing shot. A wide shot lets the viewer see what is happening as the reporter begins to tell the story. The reporter then tries to interview people involved in the event to find out more details. He or she tries to get several different people to speak so the story will be told from all points of view.

When a reporter and cameraperson go out to an event, they often videotape people at the scne of the story. Later, the reporter and cameraperson will edit all these pieces to make the TV news story, called a short package.

◀ **A student practices an on-site interview.**

Writing and Editing a Package

As reporters look at the video footage, they begin to edit out what they do not need. Some reporters may spend hours gathering information for a story but will only have a minute or so to present it. Because of this, reporters must be able to pick out the most important video footage and interviews.

It takes a lot of raw video footage ▶
to make a short final package.

19

An instructor explains the important ▲
elements to include in a demo tape.

Getting Hired

A TV station's general manager or news director is usually in charge of hiring new reporters. Reporters must have a videotape of their work—this is called a demo tape. The general manager or news director will look at a potential reporter's demo tape to see how well he or she can do a news broadcast.

A news director can tell if reporters are good writers by the way they put their demo packages together. A demo tape should be three to five minutes long. Most reporters include three short packages. These may include a serious story, a story about a local town, and an interesting feature story.

A teacher gives a student a demo
tape she helped him make. ▶

Beginning news reporters usually apply for jobs at small television stations to gain experience. These jobs usually last for two or three years. Later in their careers, TV reporters may decide to work for larger stations. Big stations usually require reporters to have a college degree, at least two years of experience, and a good demo tape.

**Daily assignments are discussed ▲
at the morning news meeting.**

On the Job

Reporters start their workday with a news meeting. At this meeting, the news director, assignment editors (people who assign stories to reporters), and other reporters go over the events of the day. They talk about news of the day, such as weather, traffic jams, and car accidents. They also talk about local events that will happen that day. Each person tells the others what he or she thinks might make a good story. During the news meeting, assignment editors give each reporter a story to work on for the day.

There are TV news stations playing in the newsroom at all times. This way, reporters can see a late-breaking news story and get to work on it too.

At News Channel 8 in New Haven, Connecticut, daytime news reporters come to work around 9:30 A.M. Many TV reporters start their day earlier than that. Many reporters watch news broadcasts during their breakfast. They also listen to news on the radio as they drive to work. This way, they can keep up with any important news.

▼ Reporters begin their day with a meeting.

Practice Being a TV Reporter

Here are some ways you can practice being a reporter

- Keep a daily diary of events.
- Interview your friends or family. Ask the six questions: Who? What? Where? When? Why? and How?
- Read your local newspaper.
- Write a fake story and tell it to your friends or family.
- Watch TV news.
- Write stories about things you notice around you.
- If you can use or borrow a video camera, you can practice shooting your own newscast.

A Typical Day at News Channel 8

After the morning meeting, TV reporters make phone calls—sometimes lots of them. Each reporter has to find places to videotape and people to interview to create a package. For example, a health reporter may be assigned a story about cancer. The reporter may decide to talk to a doctor about new ways to prevent cancer. Then the reporter may want to interview a patient to see how the treatment worked. He or she must call the local hospitals and find a doctor to interview. Then he or she needs to talk to the public relations department of the hospital to make sure the camera crew can come in to interview a patient.

▲ A reporter begins making calls.

Putting the Package Together

Once a reporter has interviews lined up, he or she works with a cameraperson (sometimes called a photojournalist) who will videotape everything. A cameraperson and TV reporter work together closely. As they drive to the interview, they talk about how best to get the story.

Once at the scene, they carry in the videotape equipment. Good reporters take time to greet their interview subjects, so they will feel comfortable on camera.

◄ A reporter and photojournalist arrive at an interview site.

26

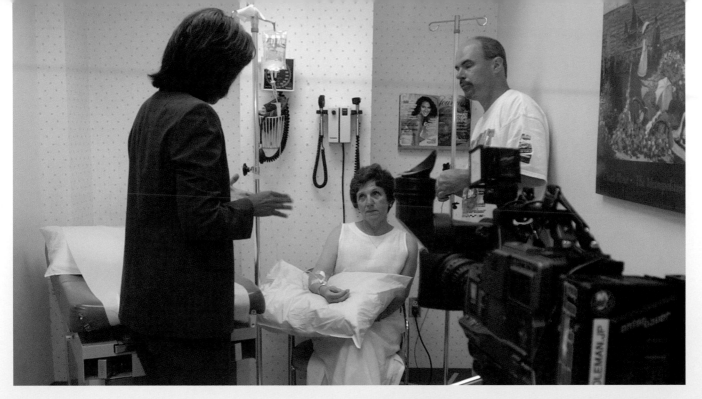

Once an interview begins, the reporter asks who, what, where, when, why, and how. The story comes together and the cameraperson captures it all on videotape.

The reporter and cameraperson try to return to the station by three o'clock. This gives them two hours to write and edit the package before the five o'clock news. The reporter looks at the best videotape the cameraperson got. The reporter may choose to focus the story around that. When they get back to the studio, the reporter sits at a computer to write the story. Then the two come together to edit the video into the package that will appear on the evening news.

Who's Who

Putting on a news broadcast takes teamwork. Even though viewers only see TV reporters, many other people help to make a newscast happen. A sound engineer checks the loudness of voices and makes sure the sound is recorded properly. A director is in charge of how each piece of a news show is recorded.

◀ **The director tells which camera angle to record.**

28

The director also talks to camerapeople. He or she tells them who to focus on, and how to frame shots. The floor director is in charge of the TV reporters and others on the set. Many other people help put each news broadcast together as well.

A student practicing how to be the floor director ▼ **(second from right) counts down to start the show.**

[***ANN***]

NEWS
CHANNEL EIGHT AT
FIVE CONTINUES
WITH THE LATEST ON
POTENTIAL PLANS TO
ATTACK IRAQ....

5:09:52 PM

1

Putting on make-up ▲

◀ **The teleprompter**

The Five O'Clock News

When it is nearly time for the news
broadcast, TV reporters finish their
packages. Then they make sure they look
good. After all, hundreds of thousands
of people may see their faces.

▲ **Field reporters will sometimes join the anchors in the studio.**

The floor director counts down and the cameras roll. Then, news anchors deliver the news of the day. They stop to introduce each TV reporter, some in the field and some in the studio. In this way, the news comes together each day. Then it's back to work to prepare for tomorrow's news!

Glossary

Anchorperson TV reporter who hosts a daily news broadcast

Demo tape Short tape that shows samples of a reporter's work

Journalism Gathering, writing, and reporting news

Package TV news story, including sound, video, and photographs

Sound bites Short bits of interviews or other video that give a lot of information in a little time

Subjects People that reporters interview

Teleprompter Machine attached to a camera that shows the words of a news story on a screen

For More Information

Books

Hayward, Donna. *Jobs People Do: A Day in the Life of a TV Reporter.* DK Publishing, 2001.

Trainer, David. *A Day in the Life of a TV Reporter.* Troll Communications, 1981.

Web sites

Making It Count: Careers: TV News Reporter
http://www.makingitcount.com/jobscareers/careers/cc_shaw.asp
Ten Steps to Becoming a TV News Reporter
http://www.thelabrat.com/jobs/careerchange/10stepstvreporter.shtml

Index